ESCAPE FROM MALDEK

GALACTIC GRANDMOTHER PAST LIFE SERIES

APRIL AUTRY

COPYRIGHT © 2020

A Rights Reserved

No part of this book shall be reproduced or transmitted in any form or by any means without prior written permission of the publisher.

No liability is assumed for damages resulting from the use of the information contained herein.

The information within this book is presented from the author's personal experience and perspective, to assist the reader's quest for spiritual enlightenment and well-being,

Neither the author nor the publisher assumes any responsibility for errors, omissions, or contrary interpretations of the subject matter herein.

Any perceived slight of any individual or organization is purely unintentional.

GALACTIC GRANDMOTHER®

https://GalacticGrandmother.com
https://info@galacticgrandmother.com

ISBN (ebook) 978-1-954785-007

ALSO BY APRIL AUTRY

Galactic Grandmother Past Life Series

ATLANTIS, JOURNEY FROM THE INNER TEMPLE

MY LIFE WITH JESUS

Galactic Grandmother Spiritual Journey Series

WORKING IN THE QUANTUM FIELD, BOOK 1 & 2

MULTIDIMENSIONAL ASPECTS - HIGHER SELVES

PROLOGUE

For many years I had reoccurring dreams of being attacked from outer space. I dreamed of seeing spaceships flying overhead, blasting us with beams of light, and I was terrified as I tried to escape.

In 1994 I moved to the high desert near Palm Springs, California, where the night sky is free from ambient light, and so clear that I could watch satellites move through the stars in the distance. One of my family's favorite past times was to sit outside on a warm night, and watch the sky. The stars were magnificent, and we often saw shooting stars and meteor showers.

After moving to the desert, and joining the sky watches, my nightmares of being attacked from outer space increased. I wondered if these dreams foretold of something that would happen in the future, and I began to look at the sky even during the day with a new curiosity.

DURING A PAST LIFE regression therapy class I see myself, feel my emotions, hear my words, conversations with others, and understand the circumstances I am in as if they were happening in the present moment.

My first spontaneous past life regression was in 1982, and surprised me when I was alone in my car. I have since experienced spontaneous past life regressions fully awake, during meditation, while in a lucid dream, and during shamanic journeys. These past life experiences are as real as any present life experiences.

When I first experienced my escape from Maldek, I did not know the name of the planet that I was on. Later I learned it was Maldek, a planet that exploded during interplanetary war, and the remnants of which became part of the Milky Way.

Escaping from Maldek to the continent of Mu, was just the beginning of approximately 1,500 years I spent reincarnating there. I loved the Lemurian culture, people and spirituality, and to this day retain strong ties to their consciousness.

By reliving past life experiences, you expand your awareness beyond this current life. You tap into your own infinite nature, and this assists you to understand your Divine origin.

My hope is that by sharing my past lives, you will be inspired to explore your own experiences. Those experiences could be exciting, sad, or thought provoking, yet they might also explain what is happening in your current life. May you find purpose, and a joy filled life along the way.

CHAPTER 1

I stood looking out the window of my mountain fortress. My home was constructed of large blocks of stone, set high on the side of a mountain, and was built to blend into its surroundings. Being a General in the military, I needed privacy and security for my family.

As I looked toward the horizon, the night sky was lit up by tall buildings burning far off in the valley below. The city had been destroyed, burned to the ground and now glowed with smoldering embers. Only the tallest buildings still had flames shooting upwards. I saw foreign ships flying over the city and knew there was no hope to recover from this. I must take my family, in a spaceship that I commanded, and flee as refugees to another planet.

I turned quickly and sprinted down the stone staircase to the family gathering room. I stood in front of the fireplace and called for my daughter.

"We must go!" I told her as she entered the room.

She looked at me with frightened eyes, and I remembered her mother's eyes just before she was killed. This war had left me a widower, and my daughter at age sixteen, responsible for her two younger brothers while I was away working. My daughter was tall like her mother, with long dark hair, and wore a white dress of soft fabric that fell to the floor.

"Where will we go?" She asked.

"Krysta," I said softly, "we must board my ship in twenty minutes. Take one bag only, and have your brothers pack a bag."

"David! James!" Krysta called out.

The boys walked into the room together, and when they saw me, ran to me with excitement.

"Pack one bag, we must leave right away!" She told them.

They looked at me with surprised expressions.

"We leave in twenty minutes!" I told them, "Pack one bag and stay with Krysta."

The boys ran out, and Krysta looked at me with tears in her eyes. I had just returned home after being gone for months, I had only walked into our house a half hour ago, and stood wearing the armor that I commanded my ship in. A vest of white tiles, over a white gown that went to my knees. I was tall, with dark hair, and a muscular build.

"Father," she said, "where will we go?"

I took a step and wrapped my arms around her. "I will take you somewhere safe."

She looked up at me.

"Go pack your bag and meet me back here." I told her, "We must board the ship and leave while we still can."

WE WERE BOARDED. Krysta, David and James were seated in the cargo area with other families, and I had instructed them to be quiet.

"Stay in your seats." I told them

The boys were excited, but Krysta was old enough to be afraid. She nervously smiled at me, and I looked over at the other passengers.

"Did everyone hear me?" I asked.

They nodded and said yes. I looked at my family again, smiled, and left to take my seat in the control room. This was not the large combat ship I usually commanded, it was a smaller ship used to explore and do research. I was confident that I could maneuver us off planet without being detected, yet there was always the chance of crossing paths with a foreign ship.

CHAPTER 2

After safely escaping Maldek, our ship moved deep into the darkness of space, and our planet looked tiny as we watched from a distance. Although we were leaving now, I hoped we might return in the future. As a war veteran, I thought that I was prepared for every probability, yet I could not have imagined the horror of what we were about to see.

Suddenly our planet exploded, and the men I shared the control room with, shouted out in anger. The shattered pieces of everything we knew and loved, were hurled into space, forming a cloud of debris. We immediately jumped into action preparing for shockwaves from the explosion, and thankfully we were far enough away, that although the ship was violently shaken, we did not receive damage.

I heard screams coming from the cargo area, and I quickly went to check on my children. People were wailing with fear, grief, and despair. Krysta was crying and holding her brothers tightly. David and James were shaken, yet not comprehending the extent of what just happened. When the families saw me, they began shouting questions.

"Is the ship safe?" "Where will we go now?"

I looked around at everyone and took in a deep breath.

"We are safe." I told them, "We did not suffer any damage to the ship."

"Where will we go?" They called out.

"We will seek asylum on another planet." I told them.

As more questions were called out, I held up my hands.

"I will keep you informed, but for now, please try to stay calm." I said.

I leaned down to my children, and told them, "I will keep you safe."

Krysta nodded and looked relieved.

AFTER BEARING witness to the atrocity our planet suffered, I received permission from the Galactic Council, to seek refuge on Gaia. Our acceptance as refugees on Gaia was conditional, in that we must comply fully with the law of the land or be expelled.

The Galactic Council instructed us to land our ship at a colony from Venus on the continent of Mu. The native inhabitants, Lemurians, are interdimensional and highly evolved. Their society is held together by universal spiritual laws, and the collective consciousness is peaceful and loving. However, the Galactic Council believed the Venusian culture was closer to our own, and would compliment our transition.

Upon our arrival, we were led directly from our ship to a healing center for examinations. We would be assessed, and receive therapies for our emotional, mental and physical needs.

We were encouraged to rest and enjoy the local foods, yet we were confined to a building next to the healing center, with adjoining park for outdoor enjoyment. Only after we were evaluated, and deemed ready to leave, would we be transported to a new location. Once we relocated, we would receive houses, food, education, and the opportunity to work.

I understood the complications that we presented, taking in refugees from a planet ravaged by war posed problems, as our psyches were damaged. Many were fearful, grief stricken, traumatized, insecure, and might act out with anger, resentment, or aggressive behaviors. Behaviors born out of strife and survival, I suspected we might be an experiment to learn if refugees from a waring planet could be rehabilitated. I knew that I was ready to change, I was ready to end the mantle of military leadership passed down to me from my father. I did not want my sons to follow in my footsteps, and I believed that a new life was possible for me, and for my children. I fervently hoped the others were ready to change, and if I had to take on a new leadership role to accomplish this, I would put forth my best efforts.

WE EXPERIENCED MANY NEW THERAPIES, some while laying on a table, some while sitting in a chair surrounded by sound and music, and my favorite became the light baths. I was told that the people here enjoy these light baths regularly, and I understood why. A large sunken tub was filled with water in the most soothing color, and the water sparkled with fine crystals. Each tub had a different shade of water in pink, blue, greens, violet, and all the other colors of a rainbow.

After taking one of these relaxing light baths, I stood with my children near the park.

"Father," Krysta asked, "when will we move into our new home?"

"Soon," I reassured her, "we are just waiting for the last people to be evaluated."

"I don't know why we can't leave," David said, "we've had our evaluations."

I looked at him and put my hand on his shoulder. "We came here as a group, and it's important for us to support each other."

"Everyone" Krysta told him, "from the ship will stay together."

David nodded his head and looked at James. "So, I'm stuck with him for the rest of my life!"

James punched David in the arm, and David ran off with James running after him.

Krysta and I laughed as we watched them go.

"I'm glad they have each other," Krysta said with a sadness in her voice.

I put my arm over her shoulder.

"I know it's been hard on you," I told her, "but I'm here now, and I'm not leaving. I want you to enjoy your life."

Krysta leaned her head on my chest. "I'm glad you're with us."

CHAPTER 3

*O*ur group was transported to a community that lived on a hillside overlooking the sea. We were greeted by a man and woman that led us on a tour and gave us information about living here.

First, we saw a large park that sprawled above the ocean. The park had walkways lined with blooming flowers, infusing the air with fragrance, and circulated by the ocean breeze. Many tables and chairs sat below the trees, inviting us to sit and enjoy the view. One side of the park had a meditation garden with benches, and a walkway that led through tall trees to two temples. One temple was designated Divine Feminine, the other Divine Masculine, although both men and women were invited to join spiritual activities in both temples. On the other side of the park is an area used for exercises, and a trail that led down from the park to a sandy cove, where the water was perfect for swimming.

Going inland from the park there are several large buildings, one being a hall which is the communication center of the community, where all work and social activities are coordinated. While some people are educated and trained for permanent occupations such as teachers or healers, others prefer to vary their work. Those people might work in the orchard or gardens, then switch to maintaining the grounds or working in the community kitchen. There is always work that needs to be done from housing to social services. People choose the work they feel called to do, whether deciding by the needs of the community, or a profession that promotes personal growth. All the community needs are provided by the residents, and every person is equally responsible. The main hall holds meetings, concerts, lectures, dances, and frequent social gatherings. Communal meals are also served here.

"Evening meals are served for everyone," the woman said, "or you can have a quiet meal at home."

"After eating, most people gather in the park," the man told us, "to watch the sunset, and enjoy the view at night. We like to play music, sing and dance."

We walked to three buildings which were schools. The schools were clean, and provided comprehensive studies that included academic, physical, emotional and spiritual education. The schools are an important community project, jointly administered by residents and the teachers.

"We regard all work and professions as equal," the woman leading our tour said, "no job or person is superior to another."

"Do you mean a person that works in the orchard," a man from my ship asked, "is equal to a healer?"

The woman nodded her head, "Yes, and equal to a priest or priestess in the temple."

"Whatever work is done to support our community is considered important and equal." The man leading the group said, "As well as those people that research, write, or perform for our entertainment."

The man continued explaining to us that most people in the community find ways to contribute to the subject matter and direction of the schools. There are teachers for all forms of exercise, as well as academic teachers. Universal spiritual laws are taught by the priests and priestesses of the temples, as well as meditation and self-reflection. Healers teach children how to work with energy and heal themselves, they learn how to grow food from people that work in the community gardens, and others teach how to care for the species we share our environment with. Art, music, singing, and dance classes are also included. The children are taught how to listen to their intuition, and learn critical thinking and decision making. The children even have teachers to assist them to become socially responsible members of the community.

"Children are the primary focus of this community," the man said, "because children are the key to consciousness evolution."

I now understood the difference between this culture and our own. They focused on the evolution of their consciousness, while we focused on surviving wars. I looked around at my fellow refugees and saw many of the parents with tears in their eyes. The realization that our children would be encouraged to grow into their highest potential, was more than we could have hoped for. Yet the biggest surprise was yet to come.

"Not all communities have children," The woman told us, "Our community chooses to experience families with children. That is why your families were settled here."

"I was told by the Galactic Council that you are from Venus." I said.

The man nodded.

"Yes. Our values and consciousness are compatible with the Lemurians, however, we have cultural differences, and live in different styles of buildings. The Council believes your group will assimilate more easily to our lifestyle."

"Thank you for accepting us." I said, "I think we will thrive in this environment."

The woman smiled, "I will explain how our families are formed," she looked around at our group, "because our children are not physically born to mothers."

I heard a collective gasp from our group. Even my mouth fell open, and we became very quiet, waiting to hear the woman's explanation.

"We provide energetic portals that attract a soul to incarnate. When two partners decide that they are ready to foster a child, there is a process of preparation. The partners are evaluated to insure they are in resonance with each other, and able to provide what a child needs physically, emotionally and spiritually. The child's room is prepared, and many people bring gifts for the child. Everyone feels very happy that a new soul will be joining us, just as we are very happy to have your children join us."

The man continued, "These preparations are considered necessary for the privilege of bringing a soul into the community. Once fulfilled, a priest and priestess along with the parents, open an energetic portal of love within the parent's home."

I didn't completely understand what we were being told. I looked around and saw others had puzzled expressions on their faces also.

"The parents will continue life as usual until a child, approximately eight years old, manifests through the portal and joins them. Following a short bonding period between child and parents, there is a community celebration to welcome the child."

It was explained to us that after we settled into our new homes, there would be a celebration to welcome our children into the community. As a parent, I looked forward to my children feeling honored with a party.

We started the tour again and walked past a healing center and other service buildings, on our way to one side of the community where the orchards and large vegetable gardens were located. After we were told about the food grown here, we walked to the other side of the community where a shallow river flowed down to the ocean. Houses were built by the orchards, the river and inland from the community buildings. There were no tall buildings, no busy streets, and when people walked by, they greeted you with smiles and introduced themselves.

"We consider everyone in the community our family." The woman said and smiled.

I had never seen such a place, and certainly never imagined I would begin a new life here. My heart swelled with gratitude that my children would be happy here. I took in a big breath of the fresh air, and felt my body relax. I wished the beloved mother of my children could be with me now. As we stood there, men and women from the community joined us, and began introducing themselves.

"We will be showing you to your homes now." The woman said,

"We have picked houses for you according to how many are in your family."

"Please go with the people that call out your names." The man said.

Our group became excited, waiting to hear our name, then leaving to see where we would live. When we heard our name, the boys jumped up and down. Krysta looked at me with a big smile.

"This is it!" I told them, "This is the beginning of our new life!"

CHAPTER 4

Our house was on the hill and had a view of the ocean, with a walkway through tall trees to reach the river. The river is a favorite spot for all the children, because the water is shallow and safe to play in. After living on the side of a rocky mountain, in a stone house, Krysta loved our new home which was built to enjoy nature. We had flowers, trees, birds, and most importantly we had peace. I spent precious time with my children and was thankful every day for this opportunity.

David and James wanted to start school immediately and were making many new friends. Krysta needed more time to adjust, yet after meeting girls her own age at the park, she decided she was ready also. I walked the children to school, then went to the community hall to meet the men and women from my ship. We had a meeting with community members about our options.

"Many of you will find work that you can do now," a man said, "others will need to decide what you want to do, and train or educate yourself for it."

I nodded and looked at the men I commanded. We had spent our lives in the military, and I hoped that we could find work suited for us here. The man looked at me.

"We have arranged a meeting for you and your men to speak with a specialist. She will evaluate your life skills, and help you find work that is satisfying."

"That is a great idea!" I said and nodded to my men.

A woman stepped forward and smiled at the group.

"You have suffered a great loss. We know that family and friends had to be left behind and were unable to escape. We want to help you, through personal counseling, and also through group sessions that are especially helpful for the children."

"Thank you." A mother from our group responded.

A woman with silver and grey hair, dressed in a long white gown, walked into the room, joined the man and woman speaking to us and they nodded at her. She turned toward us and smiled.

"Welcome. My name is Alana, and I am a priestess at the Feminine Temple. Our priest for the Masculine Temple is Artur and you will meet him there. If you would like to join me, I will take you to the temples and explain some of our services to you."

I felt excited to see inside the temples and hear about the Venusian spirituality. Many others in our group showed enthusiasm for this also, and we followed Alana from the community hall. We walked through the park and toward the meditation gardens. Alana turned and put a finger to her lips, as we passed people sitting throughout the garden meditating. We reached the Divine Feminine Temple where she instructed us to remove our shoes.

The temple was built from smooth white stone. Steps went up to double carved wooden doors, she opened a door for us, and when I looked inside I admired the beauty and serenity. There was a walkway through the center of wooden benches, that headed toward a raised wooden platform. Behind the platform was a wall of glass which looked out on a garden with flowers, a fountain, and trees.

"Please come in." Alana said, and walked toward the back of the temple.

We followed her to the platform, where she turned to face us.

"Artur and I lead meditations in both temples, we give classes and teach on many subjects. We also do spiritual counseling, and help you understand what is possible here."

I wondered what she meant by helping us understand what is possible.

"You may come here at any time. The temples are always open. Our classes and meditations are posted in the community hall, and you may schedule spiritual counseling with us there also."

I spoke up, "I am interested to learn your religion."

Alana smiled and answered in a sweet voice.

"We do not have a religion. We are here to assist you to know yourself."

"I don't understand." I told her.

"We all are spiritual beings," she said, "we help you discover that."

"I will definitely need classes and counseling!" I said.

The group laughed, with my men laughing the loudest.

"We do have spiritual celebrations that you will learn about."

I was intrigued. I wanted to know how the Venusians had achieved such a peaceful life, and I believed the answers were tied to their spirituality.

"I'll take you to meet Artur now." Alana said, and led us out of the Feminine Temple.

We walked a short distance through the trees to arrive at the Divine Masculine Temple, which looked identical to the first temple. Alana opened the door, and we went through the center isle to where a tall man stood. He wore loose fitting pants and shirt. His hair was brown with grey streaks and touched the top of his shoulders. When he saw us, he smiled, and his blue eyes shone brightly with enthusiasm.

"Welcome!" He said and stepped forward to greet us.

He was tall, like me, and his voice had a soothing tone to it.

"This is the Divine Masculine Temple, although women are welcome as well." He said. "Alana has told you the services we offer. I want you to know that we are here for you. We want to help you in any way we can."

He walked from the center of our group to stand in front of the platform and turned to point toward the window.

"We believe that we are family with all things in nature, including plants, the water, the animals, birds and fish. We honor them as co-creations of God."

He turned back to look at us and smiled again. "I'm not familiar with your spiritual beliefs," he said, "I welcome discussions with you so that I might learn."

"I would like that." I told him.

Artur nodded, "Good!"

Alana spoke up, "I will show you the temple gardens now."

She led us around the speaker's platform, to a door by the window, then out to the garden. A large water fountain stood in the center, and walkways lined with flowering bushes led away from the garden.

"The garden is shared by both the Divine Feminine and Masculine Temples." Alana told us. "We do ceremonies here, as well as inside the temples."

"What kind of ceremonies?" A woman from our group asked.

"The most common are initiations and joinings." Alana answered.

"Joinings?" The woman asked.

"When two people wish to make a formal commitment to each other." Alana said, "We say they will be joined."

"Oh!" The woman nodded, "I understand."

Alana took us back to the community hall, and showed us where the temple schedules were, and how to schedule personal spiritual counseling.

"I look forward to seeing you again." She told us before she left.

I felt an inner excitement to learn from Artur and Alana. I had spent my life learning about war, now I was free from that, and have the opportunity to learn something new. I scheduled myself to see Artur two days from now, when the children would be in school.

"You will see Artur?" One of my men said.

"I will!" I told him, "I am done with war."

"I am also." He said seriously.

I was happy that my men were finished with military duty, could spend time with their families, and pursue things that made them happy. I smiled at him, and we walked out of the hall together.

CHAPTER 5

I met the men that had been under my command in the community hall. We were to be evaluated by a woman named Seaea, so that we might find work compatible with our skills and personal dispositions. I was happy to see them, and the men looked relaxed.

"You look well." I told them. "How are you adjusting?"

"I eat, sleep and try to think what I should do next!" One man told the group.

We laughed because we were used to a lifestyle without a lot of personal choice.

"Yes!" Another said, "I feel uneasy because I do not know what I should do."

We heard a person walk into the hall, and a female voice answered him.

"I will help you with that."

We turned to see a woman walking toward us. She was beautiful, with a big smile, and I heard the men whispering under their breath about her looks.

"I am Seaea," she said, "My father loved the sea, and named me after it."

The men laughed, and I realized that she had made them feel comfortable by saying that.

I smiled at her. "My name is Larken."

She smiled and looked into my eyes.

"Your eyes are the color of the sea!" I told her, and I admired their deep blue color.

"You are the General." She said.

I felt an attraction to her immediately. I looked around and realized my men were watching us.

"I will speak with each of you," she said, "I will start with General Larken."

The men stepped back as Seaea led me across the hall to a place where we could talk privately. We sat down across from each other at a table, and I admired her long blonde hair that waved and curled around her face. Her face was sweet, and I wondered how old she was.

"I wanted to speak with you first, because you can give me your assessment of the men you commanded."

I nodded. "I know them well."

She smiled at me and again I felt strongly attracted to her.

"I want to find work that will satisfy them." I said.

Seaea looked past me to the men, "I understand that this life will be very different, and perhaps difficult for them."

"You are correct." I agreed.

Seaea took a clear glass instrument out of her bag and laid it on the table. "Let us begin."

The glass instrument came alive when she said that, and it seemed to be recording our conversation. We discussed each man, and afterwards she looked at me with an intense expression.

"What will make you happy Larken?"

The question startled me. I took in a deep breath and blew it out.

"I am happy that my children are safe and have many opportunities here."

"This is a perfect environment for children." She said.

"I never imagined such a place existed." I told her.

"Your children will be happy," she smiled at me, "what will make you happy?"

"Do you mean for work?" I asked.

"Work will contribute to your happiness, and I am sure there are many jobs you are qualified for, if you are ready for that."

"Ready?" I asked.

"It is most important that you find something that stimulates you. In our community, work comes naturally after finding your primary interests."

I must have a confused look on my face, because she continued.

"You may enjoy engineering and find work in that field, or the love of plants may draw you to work in the garden or orchard. What interests you the most here?"

"I understand what you're asking," I told her, "I am interested in learning about your spirituality, yet I cannot see how I could work in that field."

Seaea tilted her head, "Oh, that is interesting!"

"Why?" I asked.

"Because you are a General, a man that thinks in concrete terms of probabilities, yet you are interested to learn about incorporeal possibilities."

I laughed, "It does seem the opposite of being a General!"

She laughed with me and looked into my eyes.

"You should make an appointment with Artur.

"I already have." I told her.

"Good, I want to meet with you soon, and hear about this."

"I would like that." I told her, although my motivation was my attraction to her, not discussing my spiritual interests.

She stood up, and I followed her lead.

"I will speak with your men now."

THE CHILDREN WERE LEAVING SCHOOL, so I walked from the community hall to meet them.

"Can we go swimming?" David asked.

"He means in the ocean." Krysta said.

"Yes!" I said, "We haven't been there yet."

David and James jumped around and were happy.

"Our friends are going swimming." James told me.

We went home, ate some fruit and talked about our day.

"Do you have school assignments to do at home?" I asked.

"Just research on this." James said and pulled a glass instrument from his bag. It looked similar to Seaea's.

"What do you need to research?" I asked.

"Planets." James said.

"We are supposed to find Venus," David told me, "where Maldek was, and where we are now."

"Gaia." Krysta told him.

"I think that is a good idea." I said. "Krysta, do you have an assignment?"

"We are learning about the native plants." She said.

"I want you to do your assignments, then we will change and go to the cove." I told them.

David and James complained, I shook my head at them, and they looked at Krysta.

"Don't look at me!" She said and laughed.

WE WALKED down the path to the cove. Many children and adults were here, swimming in the calm water, and enjoying the sun by sitting or lying on the sand. The boys ran straight to the water and their friends, Krysta walked over to a circle of her new friends, and I looked around at the adults. I saw a hand wave at me and went closer.

"Welcome!" Seaea said.

I was very happy to see her so soon.

"Thank you. May I sit with you?"

"Yes!" She smiled and watched me sit down.

I turned to look at her. "Are you with someone?"

"No, I come here every day, to swim and enjoy the sun."

I noticed that her hair was still wet, with strands that were beginning to dry and curl. Her face was tan, and youthful without any lines around her eyes or mouth, which reminded me of Krysta. She had an important job, so I thought perhaps Venusian women look young for their age. Then I heard screams and laughter, turned to see my boys taking turns with the others, being thrown into the water.

"Those are your children?" Seaea asked.

"Yes," I answered and pointed to Krysta, "she is my daughter."

"I read your records and know their mother was lost in the war." Seaea said.

I looked back at her and wondered if knowing that was part of her job.

"Yes." I said.

"Are your children enjoying it here?" She asked.

"Very much." I answered. "Do you have children?"

"No children," Seaea said, "and no partner."

"No partner? You are so beautiful there must be many interested."

I spoke without thinking, and she looked down.

"I am sorry, I didn't mean to be so familiar with you." I told her.

She looked back up at me. "I have not found a man that I wanted to join with."

I did not know what to say, yet it made me happy that she had not joined with anyone.

"Maybe he's from another world!" I joked.

We both laughed, yet I meant what I said.

Krysta and two friends walked over, and I introduced Seaea to her.

"Can I go to the park with them?" Krysta asked, "some boys from school are going to play music soon."

I looked at my daughter, she was a young woman now, not my little girl.

"Find us in the hall for evening meal." I told her.

Krysta smiled, "Thanks!"

Seaea and I watched Krysta walk away with her friends.

"The young men that play music in the park" she told me, "are very popular with the girls!"

Seaea laughed, and I shook my head.

"Will you join us for the evening meal?" I asked her.

Seaea smiled at me, "I eat at home."

I nodded, "I am grateful that my children eat at the hall, because I am not a cook!"

"You didn't train for that!" Seaea said and laughed.

We watched the boys play in the water and spoke about my men. We agreed on many kinds of work they could do, based on their interests. She asked me about my experience when we escaped, and I saw tears in her eyes when I described seeing Maldek explode.

She shook her head. "You have seen so much."

"I have seen a lot being a General," I told her, "yet that was the worst."

"I am so sorry." She said, then reached over and placed her hand on my arm.

I looked down at her hand, then up at her.

Seaea pinched her lips together and shook her head. "I should go."

"You are leaving? Why?"

Seaea looked at me, and her face was flushed. "I, I have to go."

She grabbed her bag, stood up and walked away. I watched her leave and wondered why she left so suddenly. My thoughts were interrupted by the boys.

"We're hungry!" David and James both said.

I stood up. "I'm going to get wet first!"

I ran into the water, with the boys chasing me. We played and laughed, then ran to the sand, where we stood drying in the sun.

"Are you ready?" I asked them.

As we walked toward our house, I couldn't stop thinking about Seaea, and wondered what she thought about me. I thought that she might consider me too old, or incompatible because I was a general from another world. My hope was that she would get to know me, and develop feelings for me, as I realized I had for her.

CHAPTER 6

I left early to see Artur. I wanted to sit in the meditation garden and gather my thoughts. As I walked through the park, I looked out across the blue sea, and saw clouds over the water in the distance. The breeze gently blew off the ocean and I felt it on my face, along with the warm sun. Birds sang in the trees, and I heard children singing from the school behind me.

"What a wonderful day!" I thought.

I still felt amazed at our good fortune to have been accepted as refugees here. I reached the path that led into the meditation garden and turned to walk through the trees. I spotted a bench and sat down. I took in a slow, deep breath and closed my eyes. I smelled the flowers, and their fragrance was sweet and intoxicating to my senses. I took another slow, deep breath and felt relaxation spread throughout my body. I sat very still and observed this new experience, then I heard footsteps, and looked up to see Artur approaching me. I stood to greet him, he motioned to sit, and joined me on the bench.

"Do you meditate?" He asked me.

"This is my first attempt." I smiled at him, "not much time for it in the military!"

Artur nodded. "We do not have military here, please tell me how you became a General."

I told him of my childhood, being raised as the only child of a General, and how I was expected to follow in his footsteps.

"Was this something that you wanted?" He asked.

"I thought I did." I answered.

I told him about the military school I attended, and the advanced training I received.

"My father assembled a team that educated and coached me into the perfect military son, then fast tracked my career with his connections."

"Were you young when you began commanding?" Artur asked.

"Yes, I was really too young, yet I was self-confident, and fortunately my decisions were successful."

"You had a family along the way?" Artur asked.

I nodded. "A daughter and two sons, who are with me here."

"And their mother?" He asked.

"She was a casualty of the war and killed almost two years ago." I answered.

"How have your children adjusted?"

"Very well. My daughter is older than the boys, and she took on the role of mother while I was away at work. I employed a teacher, chef and housekeeper, so she had help."

"That is fortunate." Artur said.

I looked away at the flowers and back to Artur. He watched and waited for me to speak.

"When we took our tour," I told him, "I felt drawn to the temples. I don't know why I felt excited, I just knew that I wanted to learn more about your spirituality."

Artur nodded, "This excitement is your inner guidance, and it signals that you are ready to begin."

"Begin?" I asked.

He smiled at me. "You are ready to begin learning about yourself. Not the Larken that is a General, not the Larken that is a father. You are ready to learn who you are inside. Real knowledge is found within."

He tapped his fingers to his heart. "In your heart."

I shook my head. "This is a foreign idea to me."

Artur laughed, "We are in a foreign land!"

I laughed now, and he stood up.

"I wanted to know you better." He said, "I like your honesty."

I stood up also, "I look forward to learning from you."

"We should meet tomorrow, and I will give you some study materials." Artur said.

"Great! I'll see you tomorrow." I told him.

Artur walked toward the temples, and I sat back down on the bench. I had time before the children were finished with school, and with no job, I didn't have to be anywhere. I thought about my conversation with Artur and wondered what I would learn. Then thoughts of Seaea entered my mind, days had passed since we spoke last, and I wanted to know what happened between us. She seemed upset and I didn't know why.

"Should I try to see her at the cove?"

I wondered if I should take the children there after school. I stood, walked to where I could look down at the sand, and saw someone swimming. It was a woman.

"Is that her?" I thought.

I WALKED QUICKLY down the path and watched as the swimmer headed to the other side of the cove. Only one other person, reading a book, was on the sand. I began walking in the same direction as the swimmer, then saw the swimmer change direction and start toward shore. I sped up and recognized Seaea walking out of the water. I waved at her, and she stopped to look at me, then put her hands on her hips.

"Hello." I called to her.

When I got closer, I saw that she was not happy.

"Why are you here?" Seaea asked.

I was surprised by her reaction.

"I wanted to see you," I told her, "why are you angry?"

She looked down and shook her head, then back at me.

"We shouldn't see each other outside of work."

"Why?" I asked.

"I am here to help you," She looked at me with concern, "during your transition."

"I appreciate that, however," I told her seriously, "I am attracted to you."

"You are vulnerable now." Seaea said with a serious tone.

I took in a breath, blew it out, and spoke slowly.

"I'm not from Venus, I'm older and a warrior, so I understand."

She watched me closely, and I knew she saw my disappointment.

"There is nothing wrong with you," She said, "I would like to know you better."

I looked into her eyes and couldn't stop the big smile on my face. She stood across from me, and she appeared as a goddess. Her long hair was dark from the water, she was tall with a slender body and long legs. She continued looking at me and spoke softly.

"I must do my job. I cannot have a personal relationship with you, while I am counseling your men."

"I understand," I told her, "I respect you for this."

Seaea smiled. "Thank you."

"I will wait until you are ready."

"Good." Seaea said. "Will you walk with me?"

We left the cove, and the feeling between us, became our special secret.

CHAPTER 7

"We will be traveling to witness the Lemurian sacred birth." Artur told me.

I pulled my eyebrows together, "Sacred Lemurian birth?"

"Yes." Artur explained, "Like us, the Lemurians do not physically give birth to their children. A Lemurian princess will go through the physical process of pregnancy and birth for her people, as a sacred ceremony that represents their history."

"That is interesting." I said.

"The child that is born will continue the Lemurian royal lineage."

"Oh." I said, "Will everyone travel to see this?" I asked.

Artur shook his head, "Only priests and priestesses from the colonies may witness."

"I am going?" I was surprised.

"Yes," Artur said, "you are in training to be a priest, so you should be there."

AFTER SPENDING every day for a year learning from Artur and Alana, I had begun counseling my men because they trusted me and were receptive to my guidance. Artur sat in the room and listened, later he advised me on what he witnessed.

"You can assess people, and intuitively know how to communicate with them." He told me.

I listened carefully.

"You listen to what they say, and you understand that they may not be expressing, what they really mean or think."

I laughed. "This was a skill I needed when I negotiated as a General."

"The communication skills you learned in the military, are valuable during counseling."

Artur said, and continued, "Would you like to begin training to do this work?"

I pulled my eyebrows together. "Do you mean train to be a priest?"

Artur nodded. "Yes."

I wanted to continue my spiritual studies, and the thought of working as a priest excited me.

"Yes!" I said, "If you think I can be trained."

"Training is the smallest part of being a priest," Artur told me, "wanting to help others, and being loving and compassionate are most important."

BESIDES MY NEW training to be a priest, Seaea and I had begun our relationship. We were very happy together, and my children liked her. As I suspected, Seaea was much younger than me, and became a friend and confidant of Krysta's, such as an older sister might be. David and James thought she was pretty and nice, which was good enough for them to welcome her into our family.

Seaea told me that her parents lived in an older and larger Venusian colony that was quite far away. Several years ago, she moved after her schooling to be an occupational counselor, because there was a position available here. She had counseled mostly young adults, until we joined the community. Our group of refugees presented a unique opportunity, and she was excited about this. She would gain invaluable knowledge and experience, and had been contacted by a colleague, that was anxious to join her.

I told Seaea and my children, that as part of my training to be a priest, I would leave to witness the sacred Lemurian birth that Artur told me about.

"Don't worry about us while you are gone!" David said.

James laughed, "Don't worry about what Krysta will be doing!"

I looked at Krysta, and her face flushed.

"What information am I missing?" I asked.

"Krysta has a new friend!" James said excitedly, "a friend that wants to kiss her!"

"He does not!" Krysta protested.

"Krysta," I said calmly, "please tell me about him."

Krysta told me that he was one of the boys that play music in the park. That he was two years older than her, and that he wanted to meet her at the dance in the community hall.

"Do you like him?" I asked.

She nodded, "He is really nice."

"I want to meet him," I told her, "have him sit with us during the evening meal."

Krysta smiled, "I will tell him."

Krysta and the boys left for the community hall, it was time to eat, and I turned to Seaea.

"What do you think about this boy?"

Seaea smiled, "He is shy and uses his music to make friends, and he seems to really like Krysta."

I nodded, "I knew this day was coming."

Seaea put her hands on the sides of my face. "It will be fine."

"Will you join us?" I asked Seaea.

She sighed, "I will."

"Thank you!" I knew she didn't like the noise in the crowded dining hall. "I appreciate you."

We left my house and walked toward the community hall. I walked with my arm over Seaea's shoulders, when she suddenly stopped and looked up at me.

"I want to live with you." She said.

I wrapped both arms around her and squeezed. "I want that also."

We smiled at each other, and without saying more, continued to walk. We were happy being together, and we didn't need words to know what each other felt.

Artur, Alana and I traveled to a Lemurian village built next to the sea. A crowd of Lemurians had gathered to celebrate this sacred occasion, and they were dressed in white clothing made from a light fabric, with flowers in their hair and hanging from their necks. The Lemurians' hair was black, they wore it long, and their skin was tanned dark by the sun. We stood back amongst the crowd, behind a large water fountain, anxiously watching the door of the white temple. There were steep steps that went up to an open door, and we waited for the princess to appear.

"There!" Someone called out.

I saw a man that looked like a priest walk out first, followed by two elder women, then the princess with a woman on one side supporting her, who I thought was her mother. A young muscular man, wearing a white cloth that hung from his waist, held her on the other side. This man was very protective of her, and helped the princess walk slowly and carefully down the steps. The princess had flowers in her hair, was dressed in a white gown, with her belly swollen underneath. The crowd cheered and threw flowers toward the procession.

The priest and two elder women stood waiting at the fountain for the princess. When she reached them, the princess stood while the priest and two women took water from the fountain and blessed her with it. I had seen my children's mother prior to giving birth, and I recognized the discomfort that the princess was in. She smiled yet was in great pain.

After being blessed, the man and her mother helped the princess walk to the water's edge. The man held the princess as they slowly sat on the sand, then the princess laid back against the him, facing the water. She bent her knees, and her mother squatted down near the her, while the sea water gently rolled in around the princess's feet.

The birthing process began. The crowd was very quiet, and we watched intently as the princess strained and cried out. The princess squeezed her man's hands as she endured the pain for her people, and finally birthed the baby.Her mother washed the princess and baby in the water, then handed the baby to the man. He stood up smiling, and held the baby for all to see.

The crowd cheered loudly, throwing flowers and clapping their hands. The princess birthed a girl, who would herself, go through this when she grew older.

"We have not seen this before." Alana told me.

"We are blessed to witness it." Artur said.

I did feel blessed. The Lemurian sacred birth is a sacrifice the princess makes for her people, so that their lineage and ancestors are honored.

"The Lemurians believe their ancestors remain part of their lives. They believe their ancestors guide them, protect them, and communicate with them through the priests." Artur said.

"Thank you for taking me." I told them. "I won't forget this experience."

The Lemurian celebrations would go on for days, and we needed to return home. We walked through the crowd and I heard people playing music and singing, I smelled food being prepared and cooked outdoors, and there was much laughter. Artur found the priest and elder women, and he spoke enough Lemurian to thank the priest for allowing us to be here. Artur gave the priest a gift for the baby, then introduced me and Alana. The priest and elder women were happy to see us and very welcoming. Artur and the priest spoke for a few minutes, then Artur told us that we would leave. We said thank you and goodbye, then walked away. As we left, I observed as much as possible, so that I could tell my children and Seaea what I saw. I hoped to come back again, because the Lemurians were a happy people, and I wanted to know more about them.

CHAPTER 8

Many years have passed, my children are all grown, and I now live by myself in a small house near the temples. Krysta joined with the young musician, and they have welcomed a son into their home. They named him Larken after me, and I spend a lot of time with him. David lives with a woman and they both work in the orchard and gardens. He found his true interests lie in the natural world of plants. He is happy working outdoors, growing fruits and vegetables, and always has a smile on his face. James enjoys science, and after finishing school here, he left for a larger Venusian colony. He is in an advanced training program for interplanetary travel. My children have grown into wonderful adults. Moving to this community was the best possible outcome for my family, and the other refugee families. We have all flourished, and our gratitude for the opportunity to settle here, has been expressed in our contributions to the community.

I work as a priest, which simply means I offer support and guidance to others, during their process of self-enlightenment. I have joined Artur and Alana in giving meditations, spiritual classes, and counseling. We also mentor people that gravitate toward working in the spiritual field, and several have joined us.

I developed a program to teach at the schools about life on Maldek, and why violence is not allowed by Universal Law. I am busy with work that fulfills me, that assists my own spiritual growth, and elevates our collective consciousness. This is quite a difference from my background as a General on Maldek.

Seaea and I were happy together, raised my children, and both pursued our satisfying work. Seaea and her colleague became experts on refugee resettlement, and were asked to give lectures about what they learned at different Venusian communities, and also before the Galactic Council. Eventually, both were asked to teach in a school of higher knowledge. After much discussion, Seaea decided that she should move for this work opportunity, as it was in alignment with her personal growth, and in the same community where James and Seaea's parents live. I fully supported her, and although there was sadness about our lives going in different directions, we remain close and visit each other when possible.

I HAVE LIVED TWO LIVES. The first on Maldek, had many good experiences associated with my family, yet also had many bad experiences during my work in the military. I found fleeting happiness when I saw my family between work assignments, yet there was always an underlying stress and anxiety, knowing the potential danger for my family. And indeed, the mother of my children was lost to those dangers of war.

My second life has been one of spiritual expansion, freedom to live without fear, and a deep happiness born out of witnessing my children grow into happy adults following their interests. I am working for the benefit of others, while learning through my own experiences, and share time with my children and grandson. I am content, I have no desires for anything else, and I see a long future ahead until I am ready to leave this world.

ABOUT THE AUTHOR

April Autry

April writes about her spiritual journey, including many of her past lives.

April is an intuitive mentor, Quantum healer, Reiki master, yoga teacher, marriage minister, and teaches alignment of your mind-body-soul through consciousness expansion and spiritual practices.

Books, meditations, courses and spiritual lifestyle products can be found on her website:

GalacticGrandmother.com

April enjoys reading your book reviews, so please feel free to email her at:

info@galacticgrandmother.com

www.ingramcontent.com/pod-product-compliance
Lightning Source LLC
Chambersburg PA
CBHW061347040426
42444CB00011B/3135